Original title:

Winter's Lanterns

Copyright © 2024 Swan Charm

All rights reserved.

Author: Mirell Mesipuu

ISBN HARDBACK: 978-9908-52-071-1

ISBN PAPERBACK: 978-9908-52-072-8

ISBN EBOOK: 978-9908-52-073-5

Celestial Glimmers in the Dark

In the vast expanse, stars softly gleam,
Whispers of night in a silvery dream.
Galaxies dance in harmonious flow,
Painting the canvas where shadows grow.

The moonlight spills like a gentle stream,
Kissing the earth with a luminescent beam.
Night birds sing their melodious tunes,
While fireflies twinkle like tiny balloons.

Comets race through the velvet sky,
Chasing a legend that bids them fly.
Nebulae swirl in colors untold,
A tapestry woven with wonders bold.

Planets stand guard in their orbits wide,
Mysterious realms where dreams abide.
The cosmos whispers secrets divine,
Inviting us to wonder and shine.

So let us gaze into the night's embrace,
And find our hearts in this vast space.
For in the silence, together we spark,
With celestial glimmers illuminating the dark.

Celestial Flickers

In the velvet sky, they dance and sway,
Whispers of light, guiding the way.
Soft glows that shimmer, stories untold,
A tapestry woven in silver and gold.

Amidst the silence, their brilliance sings,
Dreams take flight on ethereal wings.
Each twinkle a promise, a flicker of hope,
In cosmic wonder, together we cope.

Through moonlit nights, they shine so bright,
Casting their spell, enchanting the night.
With every blink, they share their grace,
A celestial dance in endless space.

Twinkling Stars and Silent Nights

Underneath the vastness, stars ignite,
Their twinkling gossip fills the night.
A serene reminder, we're never alone,
In this deep expanse, we all have grown.

The air is hushed, as if to hear,
The gentle secrets whispered near.
With every shimmer, our dreams align,
In a cosmic script, the stars define.

Beneath the blanket of endless blue,
Hope is rekindled with every view.
Silent nights weave stories anew,
In twinkling stars, our souls break through.

Hushed Illumination

Glimmers of light across the dark,
Hushed illumination, a gentle spark.
Flickers of comfort, shadows embrace,
In the quietude, we find our place.

Softly the stars guide our way,
In the stillness, we learn to stay.
Moments of peace, where silence reigns,
In whispered lights, our heart contains.

Gazing above, the night unfolds,
Stories of wonder, waiting to be told.
With every glimmer, our spirits free,
In hushed illumination, just you and me.

Glistening Echoes

Echoes of light, across the expanse,
Rippling softly in the night's dance.
Glistening whispers, secrets in flight,
Capturing hearts with their ethereal light.

The stars illuminate paths yet to tread,
Guiding our thoughts, where dreams are spread.
In the quiet murmur of the universe,
Glistening echoes, a lover's verse.

As we wander beneath their gaze,
Lost in the magic, our spirits ablaze.
In celestial realms, we find our tune,
Where glistening echoes hum to the moon.

Frosted Ambiance

Whispers of winter softly creep,
Blankets of white the world does sweep.
Silent nights hold secrets near,
The frost brings magic, gentle and clear.

Candles flicker in the cold,
Stories of warmth begin to unfold.
Under the stars, the air is bright,
A frosted ambiance, pure delight.

Branches shimmer like silver lace,
Nature's art in an icy embrace.
Footprints crisscross in soft snow,
In this serene scene, time moves slow.

With every glance, a new surprise,
The beauty of winter, a feast for eyes.
As snowflakes dance in the moon's glow,
In frosted ambiance, spirits flow.

Radiant Snowfall

Glistening flakes drift from the sky,
Radiant snowfall, oh so spry.
Each flake unique, a delicate sight,
Transforming the world, day turns to night.

Children laugh, their joy on display,
With snowmen built, they play all day.
Sleds race down hills, soaring high,
In radiant snowfall, time slips by.

Trees bow low, dressed in their best,
Nature's peace brings tender rest.
As twilight falls, shadows grow long,
In the embrace of winter's song.

Warm fires crackle, stories shared,
Hearts intertwined, no one is scared.
Outside, the gentle flakes still fall,
In radiant snowfall, we find it all.

Glowing Embers of Frost

Morning light breaks through the mist,
Glowing embers of frost persist.
A landscape shimmering, pure and bright,
Awakens softly to the morning light.

Chilled air kisses cheeks so warm,
Nature's beauty in every form.
The sun peeks through, a gentle tease,
As frost melts slowly on the trees.

Stillness reigns in the winter scene,
Where every hue is calm and serene.
Each breath clouds softly in the air,
Glowing embers of frost everywhere.

Nature whispers a heartfelt song,
In this quiet moment, we belong.
As day unfolds and shadows glide,
In glowing embers, joy won't hide.

Lanterns of Ice

Crystal lanterns line the way,
Guiding us through the frosty play.
As twilight fades, a glow appears,
Lanterns of ice, dispelling fears.

They flicker softly in the night,
Chasing away shadows, bringing light.
Each glowing sphere a promise kept,
In the heart of winter, dreams are deft.

Footsteps crunch on the frozen ground,
In the silence, magic is found.
Whispers of secrets in the chilly air,
Lanterns of ice, a love affair.

As starlit skies begin to gleam,
In the stillness, we dare to dream.
Hand in hand, we walk with grace,
Under lanterns, we find our place.

Frosted Pathways

Snowflakes dance upon the ground,
Whispers soft, a muted sound.
Footprints tell a tale of old,
Stories wrapped in glimmers cold.

Trees adorned with icy lace,
Nature's beauty, a frozen grace.
Moonlight bathes the world in white,
Guiding travelers through the night.

Every step, a crunching song,
Echoes through the woods so long.
In this realm, so still, serene,
Magic thrives where frost has been.

Winds will weave a gentle tune,
Underneath the watchful moon.
Paths ahead, a mystery,
Carved in crystals, pure and free.

Echoes of the Enchanted Night

In the dark, where shadows play,
Stars above start to sway.
Whispers of the night unfold,
Echoing secrets, soft and bold.

Moonlit beams on water's face,
Drawing hearts to this sacred space.
Crickets sing a lullaby,
Underneath the velvet sky.

Dreamers wander lost in thought,
Finding truths that time forgot.
Magic lingers in the air,
In this world, where dreams can dare.

Gentle breezes softly call,
Inviting souls to rise and fall.
Through the night, their spirits dance,
Caught up in a fleeting chance.

Glistening Dreams

In the stillness of the dawn,
Glistening dreams begin to spawn.
Wonders bloom with soft embrace,
Whispers trace a hidden space.

Morning light, a gentle kiss,
Brings to life what we might miss.
Colors burst, a vibrant show,
Painting paths where thoughts may go.

Each vision, a sparkling gem,
Glows like daylight's finest hem.
Chasing hopes through fields of gold,
Stories waiting to be told.

Hearts aglow with every sigh,
Wishing stars that drift on high.
In the tapestry of dreams,
Life unfolds in glimmering beams.

Glows of Hope Amidst the Cold

Winter's chill may bring the freeze,
Yet in hearts, warmth finds its ease.
Flickers of hope, like flames, arise,
Shining bright 'neath swirling skies.

Amidst the frost, a fire burns,
Guiding souls on tender turns.
In the darkness, love shall bloom,
Chasing shadows from the room.

Every spark, a tale of light,
Breaking through the longest night.
Hope can flourish, brave and bold,
In the midst of winter's hold.

So gather close, let warmth abide,
Cling to love, let faith be your guide.
Through the cold, we'll find our way,
Together, welcoming the day.

Frosted Dawn

In the hush of morning's breath,
The world clothed in white,
Glittering jewels on every branch,
Winter's canvas, pure delight.

Footsteps crunch on frozen ground,
Echoes of a world so still,
Nature whispers, soft and warm,
Time pauses, against our will.

Sunrise paints the sky in blush,
A gentle kiss on frosted leaves,
Birds awaken, sing and soar,
A melody the heart believes.

Steam rises from our cups of joy,
As laughter dances in the air,
The beauty of this fleeting morn,
A moment filled with love to share.

Whispered Light

In twilight's soft and tender touch,
Where shadows linger near,
A gentle breeze begins to sing,
Whispers of love, ever clear.

The stars peek through a velvet sky,
As moonbeams weave their spell,
Lighting paths of dreams untold,
In the night, our hearts compel.

Each flicker tells a story grand,
Of journeys through the night,
Secrets held in silence deep,
Wrapped in the glow of whispered light.

The world outside fades from view,
In this cocoon, we find our bliss,
Every heartbeat echoes true,
In the shadows, a stolen kiss.

Nocturnal Fragrance

In the stillness of the night,
Fragrance dances through the air,
Moonflowers bloom with pure delight,
Underneath the starry glare.

Jasmine whispers in the dark,
A serenade for quiet souls,
Each scent unfolds a vibrant spark,
As nature gently consoles.

The cool breeze cradles dreams untold,
While shadows play their subtle game,
Every petal, a tale of old,
In the night, we find our flame.

Beneath this enchantment, we reside,
In a world that softly sighs,
Nocturnal fragrance, our guide,
In the stillness, love replies.

Enchanted Winter's Glow

Amidst the pine and sparkling frost,
A fairy tale in nature's hands,
Every flake, a wonder crossed,
An enchanted night, where magic stands.

Footprints lead to secret woods,
Where whispers echo, soft and low,
With every breath, the heart feels good,
In this realm of winter's glow.

Icicles hang like crystal dreams,
Beneath the silver moon's embrace,
A dance of light in cold moonbeams,
This winter world, our special place.

The air is filled with laughter's cheer,
As snowflakes twirl in gleeful flight,
In the season's charm, we draw near,
Embracing love in wintry light.

Luminescent Dreams in the Dark

In the night, whispers glow,
Softly weaving tales below.
Stars awaken, eyes so bright,
Guiding souls with gentle light.

Shadows dance, a waltz of grace,
Holding secrets in their space.
Dreams unfold like petals fair,
Caught in the moon's tender stare.

Each heartbeat sings a silent tune,
Cradled by the silver moon.
Winds carry wishes on their wings,
As the night, its magic brings.

Through the gloom, a spark ignites,
Illuminating lost delights.
In this realm where spirits tread,
Lies the promise of what's said.

Awake to dreams that shimmer clear,
In the dark, we cast off fear.
With each dawn, the shadows part,
Revealing light within the heart.

Crystalline Shadows

Glimmers caught in icy breath,
Fractured light that hints of death.
Silent crystals softly gleam,
Beneath the moon, they dance and dream.

Figures form in misty haze,
Echoes of forgotten days.
Shapes that whisper, glide and swirl,
Secrets in each icy curl.

Frosted paths where memories tread,
Veils of white o'er all that's dead.
Chill that bites but warms the soul,
Filling hearts, making us whole.

Reflections shimmer, tease the eye,
Echoing the distant sky.
In frozen realms where shadows play,
Time meanders, soft and gray.

Awake the dream from wintry rest,
In crystal light, we are blessed.
Embrace the chill, let it unfold,
As crystalline shadows turn to gold.

The Warmth of Ice

In the heart of winter's breath,
A paradox that spins with death.
Cold caress that softly warms,
Hiding comfort in its charms.

Icy fingers touch the skin,
But within, bright fires begin.
Under layers of frost and snow,
The warmth of life will gently flow.

Frozen lakes reflect the sun,
Where shadows hide, but joy's begun.
Each glimmer tells a tale of light,
In the silence of the night.

Embers glow beneath the chill,
Awakening a gentle thrill.
Dance of frost and fire entwined,
In this realm, our fates aligned.

Hold the warmth within your heart,
Let the icecraft play its part.
For even in the coldest place,
Love will find us, not erase.

Frosty Gleam

Morning breaks with frosty sighs,
Whispers shared by silvery skies.
Glistening on the blades of grass,
Nature's beauty, unsurpassed.

Every droplet, pure and bright,
Catches beams of golden light.
In the stillness, magic glows,
Painting dreams where travel goes.

Crystals form upon the trees,
Glittering in the gentle breeze.
Winter's breath, a soft embrace,
Shrouded in wonder's warm lace.

With each step, a crunch below,
Echoes of the world in snow.
Frosty gleam upon the ground,
In this silence, peace is found.

Let us wander hand in hand,
Through this beautiful, frosty land.
Where every moment, still and clear,
Holds the magic we hold dear.

Glacial Glow

Beneath the skies of endless blue,
A world of ice begins to gleam.
The shards of light with every hue,
In nature's grasp, a fleeting dream.

The frozen streams catch every ray,
Reflecting warmth from distant suns.
The shadows dance, then melt away,
In winter's grasp, the stillness runs.

With every breath, the chill we feel,
An echo of the night's embrace.
Each step upon the ice is real,
As whispers of the past we trace.

Amidst the silence, peace unfolds,
With crystalline structures pure and bright.
The tales of epochs softly told,
In glacial glow, they find their light.

Mists of Silver Light

In morning's hush, the world awakes,
A veil of mist, so soft and shy.
The silver threads of daybreak make,
A tapestry where dreams can fly.

The trees adorned with dew-kissed grace,
Whisper secrets to the dawn.
In every shadow, a tender trace,
Of dreams that linger, never gone.

As sunlight breaks, the silence fades,
While melodies in air take flight.
The gentle glow that softly wades,
Through mists that play with silver light.

A tranquil heart finds peace anew,
With every breath, the world transforms.
In nature's arms, we are a few,
Embraced by whispers, soft and warm.

Dreaming in the Snow

Beneath the blanket pure and white,
Where silence reigns and time stands still.
Each flake a dream, a pure delight,
In winter's heart, we feel its thrill.

The mountains rise with regal grace,
While stars above begin to glow.
In this enchanted, frozen space,
We find our thoughts like rivers flow.

A world transformed, a wonderland,
Where laughter echoes, joy takes flight.
Together, hand in hand, we stand,
As dreams unfold in soft moonlight.

Each step we take, the snowflakes sing,
A symphony of winter's cheer.
In dreams of snow, our spirits cling,
To moments pure, forever near.

Radiance Amongst the Pines

In forest deep, where shadows dwell,
The pines stretch high, their whispers call.
A sunbeam breaks the evening spell,
With golden hues that softly fall.

Amongst the trunks, we wander free,
As nature's breath surrounds our souls.
In every rustle, we can see,
A dance of light that gently rolls.

The air is rich with scents of wood,
While time stands still, our worries cease.
A moment's peace, as well it should,
In radiance, we find release.

With every step on mossy ground,
We hear the heartbeat of the earth.
Amidst the pines, our hearts are found,
In gentle whispers, we find worth.

Light Among the Shadows

In the dusk where dreams reside,
Flickering flames our fears abide.
Whispers weave through winding trees,
As hope ignites on gentle breeze.

Stars emerge in velvet skies,
Guiding hearts where silence lies.
Each shadow fades, a tale once told,
As warmth surrounds the weary soul.

Moments missed will reappear,
Illuminated, crystal clear.
Through every doubt, through every fight,
We stumble onward into light.

Courage springs from deepest night,
Chosen paths reveal what's right.
In the glow of every spark,
We'll find our way against the dark.

A journey shared, not made alone,
Together seeking love's sweet tone.
In shadows cast, our spirits thrive,
Through darkest hours, we will survive.

Echoes of the Chilling Wind

Beneath the moon's ethereal gaze,
The chill creeps in with ghostly ways.
Echoes call from distant lands,
Whispered tales from unseen hands.

Branches sway in gentle fright,
As shadows dance beneath the light.
Nature breathes a haunting song,
Resonating where hearts belong.

Cold winds carry stories lost,
Frosty memories, pay the cost.
Silent nights hold secrets deep,
Promises made, yet none to keep.

In the stillness, thoughts collide,
A journey taken, paths we hide.
With each gust, a sigh released,
In chilling winds, we find our peace.

Return to warmth, but carry forth,
The echoes ring with timeless worth.
A spirit roams where few have been,
In the grasp of the chilling wind.

Spark of the Solstice

Under the sun's embracing fire,
Ancient rhythms never tire.
Days stretch long, as shadows fade,
In the warmth, the world is made.

Colors bloom in vibrant fields,
Fruits of labor, nature yields.
Every heartbeat sings a song,
In this moment, we belong.

The spark ignites within our core,
A promise whispered, evermore.
As daylight dances on the skin,
Awaken dreams that lie within.

Golden rays, a soft caress,
Ignite the hearts that life had pressed.
In the twilight's golden glow,
The spark, our guide, begins to grow.

Celebrate the life we share,
In every breath, in every care.
Let the solstice mark our fate,
With love and light, we resonate.

In The Glow of Nightfall

As the sun dips low and sighs,
Night unfolds its velvet skies.
Stars emerge, a twinkling sea,
Whispers blend with mystery.

Moonlight dances on the ground,
Soft and silent, all around.
Dreams awaken, shadows play,
In the glow, we drift away.

Stories written, yet untold,
Moments gathered, memories bold.
Beneath the watchful night's embrace,
We find our peace in time and space.

Each breath taken, softly shared,
In this stillness, we've prepared.
Hearts beat gently in the dark,
As night bestows its sacred spark.

Let's wander where the starlight streams,
And lose ourselves in whispered dreams.
In the glow of night's sweet call,
Together, we can rise or fall.

Shivering Radiance

In the dawn's soft embrace, light plays,
A dance of shadows in gentle rays.
Whispers of morning brush past the trees,
With glimmers of hope upon the breeze.

Golden hues stretch and begin to bloom,
Chasing away the remnants of gloom.
Each pause holds the promise of the day,
As shivering radiance finds its way.

In the stillness, the world waits in grace,
For the sun's kiss to warm every space.
Life awakens with a vibrant sigh,
In the canvas of pregnant, blue sky.

Nature unfolds her intricate art,
Inviting each spirit to play a part.
Colors burst forth in jubilant cheer,
In the glow of a moment, crystal clear.

Through valleys and hills, the light will glide,
Unveiling the beauty that lives inside.
The pulse of the morning, a sweet serenade,
In the shivering radiance's warm cascade.

Ethereal Flames in the Frost

In the grip of the winter's harsh breath,
Frosted whispers tell stories of death.
Yet amidst the chill, a flicker remains,
Ethereal flames dance on invisible chains.

They twinkle like stars against night's face,
Warming the world with their fervent grace.
In the silence, warmth calls from afar,
Lifting our hearts like a bright morning star.

Illuminated echoes of passion's spark,
Gliding through shadows where visions embark.
Each flame a beacon, a tale to ignite,
In the heart of the frost, an inviting light.

Melting the ice that encases our fears,
Bringing forth laughter, banishing tears.
Through the cracks of the cold, we see the rise,
Of ethereal flames that illuminate skies.

So gather these embers, let them entwine,
Through the frost, let their brilliance shine.
For in every winter, a fire still thrives,
Ethereal flames that remind us we're alive.

Navigation of the Night's Glimmer

Beneath a cloak of velvet skies,
Stars weave tales that never die.
Guiding lost souls on their quest,
In the navigation of night's behest.

Moonlight spills like silver thread,
Illuminating paths we tread.
The night whispers secrets soft and low,
In the glimmer of stars, we learn to grow.

Each flicker a compass, a sign to trust,
Mending the dreams left in the dust.
Through darkness we wander, finding our way,
In the night's embrace, we choose to stay.

The shadows may dance, but so do we,
In the stillness, we find jubilee.
With every heartbeat, a spark anew,
Guided by glimmers that pull us through.

So sail on the winds of the twilight breeze,
Beneath the cosmos, with delicate ease.
For in the night's glow, we find our light,
Navigating glimmers that banish the night.

Frosted Echoes

In the silence of winter's embrace,
Frosted echoes leave a trace.
Each breath a whisper, cold and bright,
Painting the world in shimmering white.

Beneath the branches, snowflakes fall,
Creating a blanket that covers all.
In the stillness, the heartbeats slow,
As nature's beauty begins to show.

Footsteps crunch on a frosty ground,
In each sound, the magic is found.
Echoes of laughter, warm and near,
Dance through the chill, soft and clear.

We gather around the hearth's warm glow,
Sharing stories as the cold winds blow.
In the flickering light, shadows play,
As frost's embrace welcomes the day.

Embrace the whispers of the night,
In frosted echoes, find your light.
For every chill that the winter brings,
Holds layers of warmth in hidden things.

Radiant Cold

Chilling winds whisper softly,
Underneath the silver moon,
Stars like diamonds in the night,
Nature holds a breathless tune.

Icy branches gleam and glow,
Painting silence in pure white,
Footprints trace a soft hello,
In the velvet cloak of night.

Crystal lakes reflect the skies,
Frost lace dresses every tree,
Whispers weave through frostbitten sighs,
Binding earth and air in glee.

In this realm where dreams do dwell,
Time feels different, slow and free,
Each heartbeat casts a magic spell,
In the sparkling harmony.

Awake and breathe this frosty sight,
Embrace the cold, let it unfold,
In radiant hues and peaceful night,
We find the warmth in radiant cold.

Luminous Journeys Through the Snow

Footsteps crunch on snow so bright,
Luminous paths beneath the stars,
In the glow of winter's light,
Wonders dance from afar.

Whispers echo through the trees,
Tales of journeys yet to start,
Every flake on gentle breeze,
Sings a song that warms the heart.

Pine trees draped in winter's gift,
Branches bow beneath the weight,
Nature's touch, a spectral shift,
Guides us through the quiet gate.

Candles flicker in the night,
Mapping dreams on shadows' shore,
Guiding souls with softest light,
To explore forevermore.

In this world of white so pure,
We find the spark that leads us home,
Through luminous trails, our hearts endure,
In the magic, we freely roam.

Fireflies in Frost

In the stillness of the night,
Frosty air begins to sing,
Fireflies dance in gentle light,
Painting dreams on winter's wing.

Each glow a whisper of the past,
Stories woven in the air,
Moments held, forever cast,
In a blanket, soft and rare.

Frozen lakes like mirrors gleam,
Reflecting whispers of the stars,
In this place, we chase the dream,
Hoping to heal all our scars.

While the world wears its icy coat,
Fires of hope still brightly burn,
In the heart, a single note,
Of love that waits for our return.

So we weave these luminous threads,
In the frost, where fireflies roam,
In our dreams, where warmth still spreads,
We'll always find our way back home.

Beacon of Solitude

In the quiet shadows fall,
A beacon glows, a distant light,
Echoes of a silent call,
In the depths of the cold night.

Solitude, a gentle friend,
Cradling thoughts that softly rise,
In the stillness, we can mend,
Healing wounds with whispered sighs.

Stars above a watchful gaze,
Guiding dreams with tender grace,
In the dark, our minds ablaze,
We forge a path, we find our place.

Each breath a spark in the night,
Illuminating what we seek,
In solitude, we find our might,
In stillness, we softly speak.

As the world spins far away,
This beacon holds the heart's embrace,
In solitude, we learn to stay,
Finding grace in time and space.

Embered Paths of Remembered Glow

Flickers dance in the twilight haze,
Whispers lost in the evening blaze.
Footprints fade on the warming ground,
Stories of old in soft light found.

Memories linger like shadows cast,
Tales of a journey, shadows past.
Each ember holds a spark divine,
Lighting the soul with a gentle sign.

Paths unwound in the fading dusk,
Dreams once vibrant beginning to husk.
Yet in those glimmers, hope is born,
Guiding the heart through the night's scorn.

As echoes fade into the deep,
Light from embers begins to seep.
A warmth that wraps the silent night,
Reminding us all of love's pure light.

Together we tread through twilight's grace,
Each step, a memory we embrace.
Along these paths our spirits roam,
In embered glow, we find our home.

Silent Watchers of the Night

Stars arise in the velvet sky,
Silent watchers as time slips by.
Moonlight weaves through the whispering trees,
Carrying secrets on the gentle breeze.

Eyes gleam bright from the astral heights,
Guardians of dreams on tranquil nights.
With every twinkle, a story unfolds,
Of ancient tales and futures untold.

The world below in serene stillness,
Bathed in peace, free from ill-will.
Shadows flicker in the soft glow,
Holding truths that we yearn to know.

In this vast canvas, silence reigns,
Echoing softly like gentle rains.
Each drop a whisper, a touch of grace,
Leading us through the cosmic space.

So let us gaze at this night adorned,
By silent watchers, forever warmed.
In their presence, our spirits rise,
Beneath the blanket of endless skies.

Shining Spheres in an Icy Realm

In a kingdom of frost, the spheres gleam bright,
Crystals shatter in the pale moonlight.
Each orb a wonder, a world of its own,
Tales of the winter with stories sown.

Glistening landscapes of shimmering white,
Whispers of magic within the night.
In the icy realm where silence falls,
Shining spheres echo the winter's calls.

Their brilliance contrasts the shadowed ground,
In each reflection, a truth is found.
Frosty breath dances in the air,
As hearts beat soft in the cold's snare.

Together we wander through fleeting dreams,
In this enchanted world, nothing seems.
Bound by the shimmer, entranced we stay,
Lost in a maze where the spirits play.

So let the shining spheres guide our way,
Through the icy realms where wonders lay.
In their light, we find warmth anew,
In the heart of winter, so bright and true.

Dim Embers of Solitude

In the quiet chambers where shadows creep,
Dim embers flicker, secrets they keep.
Lonely whispers in the stillness dwell,
Casting flickers where silence fell.

Each spark a memory of days gone by,
Echoes of laughter, a soft goodbye.
In solitude's grip, the heart learns to sing,
Finding solace in the warmth they bring.

Yet darkness lingers like a faded dream,
Hope flickers softly, a fragile beam.
In the solitude, connections seem lost,
But each ember holds light, no matter the cost.

Time moves slowly, the night stretches wide,
In this embrace, our fears must abide.
But in dim embers, we glimpse the fire,
A flicker of passion, a hidden desire.

So let us wander in this quiet night,
Where dim embers shine, casting soft light.
In solitude's depth, we find our core,
In the heart of stillness, we learn to soar.

Frost-Kissed Glow

In the hush of night's embrace,
Snowflakes dance with gentle grace,
Stars like diamonds start to gleam,
Wrapped in winter's crystal dream.

Whispers of the icy breeze,
Rustle through the frost-kissed trees,
Moonlight weaves a silver thread,
A tapestry where dreams are led.

Each breath hangs in the night's air,
Frosted patterns everywhere,
Nature holds its breath in awe,
In this pristine winter straw.

Crickets quiet, night stands still,
Echoing the distant chill,
A world transformed in quiet glow,
Beneath the blanket of the snow.

As dawn approaches, shadows shift,
Frosty jewels begin to lift,
In the light, the beauty flows,
Beneath the sun's warm, tender nose.

Shimmering Whispers in the Void

In the silence, stars align,
Echoes shimmer, softly twine,
Thoughts like comets race through space,
Fleeting dreams we can't replace.

Between the notes of cosmic song,
Woven threads, where hearts belong,
Secrets drift on lunar tides,
In the void, where love abides.

Galaxies in twilight's fold,
Stories of the brave and bold,
Wishes whispered like the breeze,
Carried on the night's decrees.

Each heartbeat marks a path unknown,
In the dark, we're never alone,
With every breath, the cosmos sighs,
Endless tales beneath the skies.

Fleeting shadows dance and fade,
In the dusk, our dreams are laid,
Amidst the stars, we find our voice,
In the void, the heart's sweet choice.

Candlelight Against the Chill

Flickering flames in silent night,
Casting warmth, a tender light,
Shadows play upon the wall,
Echoes of the heart's soft call.

The world beyond feels far away,
In this glow, where dreams can stay,
Each candle, a whispered prayer,
Holding close the love we share.

Against the chill, we find our way,
Guided by the flicker's sway,
Memories wrapped in soft embrace,
In the quiet, we find our place.

Outside, the frost begins to creep,
In our hearts, the warmth we keep,
Together, we face the night,
In the glow, we find our light.

Candlelight, a soft refrain,
Dancing thoughts like falling rain,
In this moment, time stands still,
With love, we conquer every chill.

Nocturnal Radiance

In the depths of midnight's cloak,
Stars awaken, softly spoke,
Moonlit paths begin to gleam,
Guiding souls through whispered dreams.

Waves of silence, gentle tides,
In the dark, where magic hides,
Each glimmer paints the night anew,
With rays that bring the heart to view.

Nature stirs beneath the glow,
Softly breathing, whispers flow,
Creatures flit in shadowed light,
Tales unfold in the still night.

Every moment, bright and rare,
Journey shared in dreams we dare,
With every shimmer, love's embrace,
In nocturnal radiance, we trace.

As dawn approaches, soft and bright,
We hold the glow, the fading light,
In the warmth of day, we know,
The night will come, again to show.

Glimmers of the Chill

Soft whispers in the night,
Moonlight dances on the snow,
Stars twinkle with delight,
In the silence, magic flows.

Frosted branches, silver lace,
Nature's beauty on display,
In the stillness, find your space,
Let the heart be led astray.

Crisp air tinged with a breath,
Awakens thoughts both sweet and bold,
Memories weave with winter's depth,
As shadows wrap the world in cold.

Gentle flakes begin to fall,
A quilt upon the Earth will lay,
Each unique, they heed the call,
Of winter's artful ballet.

So wander through this frozen scene,
Embrace the chill with open arms,
For in this world of white so clean,
Lies the beauty of nature's charms.

Illuminated Stillness

In the hush of winter's breath,
The world is cloaked in quiet grace,
Stars above in frozen depth,
Illuminate the velvet space.

Snowflakes whisper as they land,
Painting dreams on barren ground,
Footsteps soft, a gentle hand,
Guiding silence all around.

Every shadow softly glows,
Wrapped in blankets, dark and light,
Nature's song in silence flows,
A harmony of day and night.

Through the trees, the moonlight streams,
Casting silver over all,
In this stillness, life redeems,
And shadows gently rise and fall.

Here we pause, let time suspend,
A moment rich, a breath so deep,
In this calm, our souls can mend,
And find the peace that we still seek.

Embrace of the Cold

Winter wraps the world so tight,
In its arms of frosty breath,
Crystalline beauty, purest light,
Echoes softly of life's depth.

A breath reveals the air so clear,
Kissed by frost, it sparkles bright,
Nature whispers, drawing near,
In the cold, there's warmth tonight.

Gathered 'round the crackling flame,
Hearts connect, the spirit glows,
In the chill, we find our name,
In the embrace, where love still flows.

Vistas wide, the landscape sleeps,
Nestled deep beneath the snow,
In this quiet, promise keeps,
Of springtime's kiss, the warmth will grow.

So let us dance in winter's chill,
With laughter bright against the night,
For love's embrace is strong and still,
In every shiver, pure delight.

Radiance in the Frost

Morning breaks with golden hue,
Frosted fields begin to wake,
Every blade a crystal view,
In the light, the cold can shake.

Beneath the trees, the shadows play,
A canvas bright with sparkling frost,
Nature's art in bright array,
Of every moment that we've lost.

We trace the paths of winter's breath,
Where silence speaks in softest tones,
In its clutch, life honors death,
Deep reflections, ancient bones.

As the sun begins to rise,
The chill retreats, revealing dreams,
And under sapphire painted skies,
Radiance flows like silver streams.

So let us cherish each bright spark,
In the frost, a fleeting glimpse,
Of life anew, in light and dark,
Awakening in daylight's lilt.

Serenity in the Silvery Cold

The world lies still beneath the snow,
Whispers of silence gently flow.
Moonlight dances on the frozen lake,
Peaceful dreams begin to awake.

Trees wear coats of crystal white,
Stars twinkle in the deep, dark night.
Breath of winter, crisp and bright,
Nature's beauty, pure delight.

Footsteps crunch on this winter's ground,
In every sound, a solace found.
Frosted air wraps around my soul,
Warming whispers make me whole.

The stillness fills the heart with grace,
In this moment, I find my place.
Serenity flows from the sky above,
Embracing me in winter's love.

Glimmers of Hope in the Haze

Through the mist, a light breaks clear,
A whisper soft, a promise near.
In shadows thick and clouds that weep,
Glimmers of hope awaken sleep.

With every sigh, the dawn will rise,
The sun will chase away the lies.
In the haze, dreams come alive,
With strength renewed, we will survive.

Each step forward, a chance to mend,
In tangled paths, we find a friend.
Hope's gentle touch ignites the way,
Brightening each and every day.

Through the storms, the courage grows,
In the shadows, resilience flows.
With hearts aglow and spirits wide,
We journey forth, hope as our guide.

The Luminary's Lullaby

Night drapes softly over the land,
A lullaby sung by gentle hands.
Stars twinkle, weaving dreams so bright,
Guiding lost souls through the night.

In the hush, a melody plays,
Whispers of warmth in the cool moon's gaze.
Each note a promise, soothing and deep,
The luminary sings, lulling to sleep.

Crickets chirp, a symphonic tune,
The dance of shadows beneath the moon.
With every breath, the night unfolds,
Stories of magic in silence told.

Embrace the stillness, let worries cease,
In this lullaby, find strength and peace.
The luminary shines, a beacon bright,
Cradling dreams in the velvet night.

Beneath the Frosted Canopy

Underneath branches laced with ice,
Wonder hides, a treasure so nice.
Nature's quilt, a frosty embrace,
Whispers of winter in every space.

With each soft step, the crunching sound,
Echoes of magic, all around.
The canopy sparkles in morning light,
A breathtaking view, a stunning sight.

Glimmers of joy in the frigid air,
The beauty of winter beyond compare.
Laughter dances in the crisp breeze,
Time seems to slow, inviting ease.

In this realm, the heart finds peace,
An escape from worries, a sweet release.
Beneath the frost, I feel so free,
Wrapped in the love of nature's decree.

Illuminated Frost

Under moonlight's gentle kiss,
Frosty whispers dance and play.
Each crystal holds a hidden bliss,
Nature's art in bright array.

Breath of winter, crisp and bright,
Sculpting dreams in silver white.
Every flake a spark of light,
Glistening in the cold, clear night.

Time stands still in icy gleams,
Frozen wonders, silent screams.
Memories held in frosty seams,
A world alive with whispered dreams.

Branches wear their icy crowns,
Sparkling in celestial frowns.
Nature's silence softly drowns,
Heartbeats echo in snowy towns.

In a realm of winter's grace,
Ethereal beauty finds its place.
Frosted landscapes, swift embrace,
Illuminated, time does race.

Glacial Ember

Ice and fire in dance collide,
Embers glow like secret stars.
In the chill, warmth does reside,
Bold against the night's cold bars.

Through frostbit branches, shadows creep,
Glowing hints of warmth arise.
Where ancient tales of warmth still seep,
A soft passage to the skies.

Whispers of warmth in glacial air,
Flickering sparks in frozen streams.
Light weaves through icy, bleak despair,
A bridge of wonder, woven dreams.

Each spark mirrors the starlit night,
Reflecting worlds both near and far.
In the gloom, embers take flight,
Guiding hearts like a distant star.

So tread lightly on this frost,
Find the warmth that can't be lost.
In glacial beauty, count the cost,
For every ember, love embossed.

Ethereal Beacons in the Snow

Beneath the stars, in silver glow,
Beacons shine where shadows play.
Guiding souls through chilling flow,
Crystalline paths show the way.

Each light a story yet untold,
Whispers carried on the breeze.
In the silence, mysteries unfold,
Ethereal lanterns bring us ease.

Kisses of frost upon the ground,
Twinkling charms in winter's embrace.
Through the silence, hope is found,
Casting warmth in every space.

Softly glistening, the night reveals,
Moments frozen yet alive.
Where the heart in stillness feels,
Ethereal beacons dare to thrive.

In this realm of soft, pale light,
Wonders beckon with each breath.
Guiding through the endless night,
A dance of life beyond of death.

Night's Soft Embrace

In the quiet of the night,
Whispers fold the world from sight.
Stars pull blankets from above,
Wrapping dreams in tender love.

Moonlight spills in silver streams,
Kissing cheeks with softest gleams.
Night enfolds the weary heart,
Promising a brand new start.

Crickets sing a lullaby,
Gentle breezes softly sigh.
In this stillness, fears subside,
Wrapped in night, we gently bide.

Each shadow dances, kisses air,
Magic spun from dreams laid bare.
Night's embrace, a soothing balm,
Cradling the world, sweet and calm.

Underneath the softest veil,
Where lullabies of starlight sail.
In this moment, love prevails,
As night's soft embrace gently trails.

Tranquil Flare of the Frost

In the hush of winter's breath,
Stars shiver in the night,
Moonlight dances o'er the ground,
Casting shadows, soft and bright.

Gentle flakes begin to fall,
A quilt forms without a sound,
Blankets white embrace the trees,
Nature's peace, a treasure found.

Winds whisper secrets of the cold,
Through branches bare, they weave and sway,
A tranquil flare ignites the dark,
Embers of the frost at play.

Crystalline crystals, pure and clear,
Reflecting dreams of winter's song,
Each breath a plume in the still,
In icy realms, where hearts belong.

Glowing Petals of an Icy Flower

Petals gleam in morning light,
Shimmering with frosty grace,
Nature's jewels in the chill,
A secret world, a tranquil space.

Delicate blooms of crystal white,
Embraced by winter's tender care,
Whispers of a faded warmth,
In the stillness, dreams laid bare.

Branches bow with heav'nly frost,
Each moment, a fleeting chance,
The icy flower softly glows,
In nature's silent, graceful dance.

Time drips slowly, like the dew,
On petals kissed by dawn's first light,
A reminder of love's soft touch,
In the cold, everything feels right.

Faint Flames Amidst the Snow

In the stillness of the night,
Faint flames flicker through the white,
Whispers of warmth that still remain,
Amidst the snow, a sweet refrain.

Coal-black skies hold secrets tight,
Yet in the dark, a spark ignites,
Hearts aflame beneath the chill,
Finding warmth in winter's will.

Embers dance on chilly winds,
Spirits rise, despite the freeze,
Faint flames glow, a hint of light,
A beacon bright that warms with ease.

Snowflakes swirl in graceful arcs,
As warmth and cold begin to weave,
A tapestry of joy and pain,
Faint flames flicker, hearts believe.

Whispered Lights in the Frozen Air

Bright whispers echo in the night,
As stars align with dreams of light,
In frozen air, they softly glide,
Guiding souls through winter's tide.

Secrets wrapped in silken glow,
A tranquil rhythm, soft and slow,
The universe, a canvas bright,
Painting paths with whispered light.

Footprints linger, lost in time,
Illuminated by a chime,
Winter's breath, a gentle song,
Where hearts remember they belong.

The night unfolds, a tender art,
Whispered lights ignite the heart,
Through frozen whispers, dreams take flight,
In the depth of winter's night.

A Flicker in the Frost

In the stillness of the night,
A candle dances bright,
Its glow against the chill,
A flicker, soft and slight.

Whispers of the winter air,
Carrying dreams of old,
Each shimmer holds a tale,
Of warmth in the cold.

The stars, they blink in unity,
Echoing the flame's embrace,
While shadows waltz on ground,
In their delicate race.

Crystals form with gentle grace,
Reflecting silent wishes,
A fleeting glimpse of hope,
In frost's tender swishes.

In every breath the night beholds,
The magic whispers clear,
A flicker in the frost shines bright,
Dissolving all the fear.

Serene Silhouettes

A horizon framed in dusk,
Where colors softly blend,
Shadows stretch and linger long,
In silence, they descend.

Trees standing tall and still,
Carved against the sky,
Their branches whisper secrets,
As the evening breathes a sigh.

A gentle pond reflects the hues,
Of twilight's warm embrace,
Embracing every silhouette,
In nature's calm space.

In the distance, mountains loom,
Guardians of the night,
Their peaks kissed by the fading sun,
In fading shades of light.

Each moment slips in serenity,
The world finds peace tonight,
In the dance of shadows and light,
Through whispers of twilight.

Frostfire Reflections

In the dawn's soft murmur,
A mirror shows the past,
Frostfire kisses tender blooms,
In beauty, they are cast.

Twirling sparks of ice and flame,
Where two worlds intertwine,
Each moment holds a secret,
In the chill so divine.

Reflecting on the frozen ground,
The colors softly sway,
Frost and fire in unity,
In a delicate ballet.

Nature's canvas, vivid hues,
A tapestry unfolds,
Frostfire glimmers, fleeting dreams,
In whispers it beholds.

With every breath, the magic flows,
In a dance just begun,
Frostfire reflections glow so bright,
A journey just for one.

Shadows of Light and Ice

A world wrapped in gentle frost,
Where shadows softly creep,
In the glow of morning light,
Secrets lull and sleep.

Silhouettes of towering pines,
Stand silent in the day,
Guardians of a winter tale,
In their own quiet way.

Each heartbeat of the earth,
Dollar signs of crystal sight,
As sunlight smiles with glee,
Weaving shadows through the light.

In the whisper of the breeze,
Echoes of laughter rise,
Where light and ice coexist,
Beneath the endless skies.

Embrace the beauty all around,
In moments, soft and rare,
For shadows of light and ice,
Immerse us in their care.

Shards of Light in Quietude

In the stillness of the dawn,
Soft whispers float on air.
Gentle rays paint the morn,
Awakening dreams laid bare.

Through leaves, the sunlight peeks,
Dancing with dew on grass.
Nature's smile softly speaks,
As time begins to pass.

Echoes of the world retreat,
Crickets still their song.
In this calm, I find my seat,
Where my thoughts belong.

A canvas stretched with grace,
Colors blend and swirl.
In this quiet, sacred space,
Life begins to unfurl.

Moments breathe, they take their flight,
While shadows softly play.
Cradled in this shards of light,
I lose myself, I stay.

Glistening Hues of the Deep

Beneath the waves, a world concealed,
Glistening greens and blues.
Secrets of the ocean revealed,
In this realm I choose.

Coral gardens sway and twist,
Home to creatures rare.
Every shimmer, a soft kiss,
Whispers in the air.

Fishes dart like fleeting trains,
Through shadows and through light.
Life pulses in rhythmic veins,
A dance both dark and bright.

Each current tells a tale untold,
History lost in time.
Here in the depths, bold and cold,
I find my silent rhyme.

Glimmers of life paint the floor,
Mysteries beckon near.
In these hues, my spirit soars,
Embracing every fear.

Hearthfire Reflections

In the glow of amber light,
Stories weave through air.
Crackling logs bring warmth to night,
Moments shared with care.

Flickering flames dance and sway,
Casting shadows long.
In their embrace, we drift away,
To the heartbeats of our song.

Echoes of laughter fill the space,
Love lingers in the heat.
Each smile holds a tender trace,
Memories bittersweet.

Outside, the world may freeze,
While we gather near.
Wrapped in warmth, we find our ease,
In the hearthfire's cheer.

As the night wraps soft and tight,
We cherish moments rare.
In the glow of this sweet light,
Friendship's flame lays bare.

Chasing Shadows of Sparkling Nights

Underneath the silver sky,
Stars twinkle, bold and bright.
We run, just you and I,
Chasing shadows through the night.

Moonlight casts a silver sheen,
Whispers swirl like dreams.
In this realm, so calm, serene,
Nothing's ever as it seems.

Every step reveals a spark,
Adventure in the dark.
With each laugh, we leave a mark,
A silent, glowing arc.

Time dissolves, we lose the day,
In these hues, we dive.
Captured in this endless play,
We feel so very alive.

As night unveils its magic store,
We dance with shadows bold.
In the chase, we long for more,
In these tales, our hearts unfold.

Frosty Twilight

The sun dips low, a distant glow,
Chill winds whisper secrets slow.
Stars emerge, in icy grace,
Night's embrace, a quiet space.

Trees stand tall, their branches bare,
Moonlit dreams float in the air.
Snowflakes dance in twilight's hand,
Nature's beauty, softly spanned.

Shadows stretch across the ground,
In the stillness, peace is found.
Frosty breath upon the eaves,
A tranquil heart that gently believes.

Through the night, a calm prevails,
Winter's story softly trails.
In this hush, life finds its way,
The frosty twilight holds the day.

As morning breaks, the world ignites,
Colors splash, a vivid sight.
Yet in the chill, the twilight stays,
Whispering of quiet days.

Hushed Luminescence

In the stillness, light unfolds,
Whispers of night, in silver molds.
Stars flicker soft, like candle's glow,
In this moment, time feels slow.

Moonlit paths through shadows weave,
Each breath a gift, we dare believe.
The glow of night, a gentle balm,
Wrapped in peace, our hearts feel calm.

Hushed voices dance in twilight's grace,
A sacred bond we embrace.
The world outside fades from view,
In this light, we find what's true.

With every flicker, dreams take flight,
Carried softly into the night.
Luminous whispers all around,
In this hush, true joy is found.

As day will break, the shadows wane,
Yet this light will still remain.
A memory of a time so bright,
In our hearts, a warm delight.

Distant Warmth

Across the field, the sun does rise,
With golden rays that touch the skies.
In the distance, warmth is near,
A soft embrace, a quiet cheer.

Through winter's chill, we seek the glow,
A beacon bright, in white and snow.
The world awakens, breathing slow,
In tender light, our spirits grow.

Branches bare, yet dreams ignite,
Hope blossoms in the morning light.
With every step upon the frost,
We find the warmth that wasn't lost.

The distant sun, a guiding star,
Reminds us all of who we are.
In every heart, a spark resides,
Distant warmth, where love abides.

As shadows fade, the day begins,
Each breath a promise, each laugh a win.
In the sunlight, we shall dance,
Embracing warmth, life's sweet romance.

Flickers on the Ice

On frozen lakes, the light does dance,
A shimmering sheen, a fleeting chance.
Each flicker bright, a whispered song,
In this moment, where we belong.

The wind's soft breath, a gentle caress,
Nature's magic in its express.
Ripples shimmer, reflecting dream,
As if the world glows at the seam.

Bold steps echo on the glassy floor,
A playful journey to explore.
With laughter bright and hearts so free,
Flickers on the ice, joy's decree.

Closed eyes see the beauty near,
In every glimpse, we hold so dear.
The light we seek within our soul,
Flickers on the ice, making us whole.

As shadows lengthen, day departs,
Carrying warmth in tender hearts.
We cherish moments, pure and bright,
Flickers on the ice, our guiding light.

A Caterwaul of Clarity

In the hush of the night, whispers grow,
Familiar echoes in the moon's soft glow.
A scream breaks the silence, sharp and clear,
Lost in the shadows, I linger near.

The streets wear a shroud, cloaked in fog,
Each corner hides stories, forgotten and bogged.
With each caterwaul, clarity calls,
I chase after visions as reason falls.

A crescendo of memories, tangled in flight,
They swirl like leaves in the pale twilight.
Embrace the chaos, the cacophony sings,
Within the storm, the heart truly clings.

The night bears witness to souls that roam,
Each pang of sorrow is tied to a home.
From starlit alleyways to skies of deep blue,
Caterwauls blend dreams with the anguished dew.

In the end, we find solace in cries,
In the dance of clarity beneath midnight skies.
With every sound, a story unfurls,
A caterwaul's echo, the truth of our world.

Frosty Flickers of Nostalgia

Time slips like snowflakes on fingertips,
Caught in the moment, a gentle eclipse.
Frosty flickers of days gone by,
Whisper of laughter, a bittersweet sigh.

The hearth crackles softly, warmth in the chill,
Muffled memories twinkling, a soft, gentle thrill.
Childhood echoes in the midnight air,
Moments of magic, ensnared with care.

In the silver moonlight, shadows play games,
Fleeting reflections, like familiar names.
Each glimmering glance, a time traveler's call,
Frosty flickers dancing, enchanting us all.

Embers of yesteryear glowing bright,
Wrapping us warmly through long winter nights.
Nostalgia's embrace, a cloak we wear tight,
Flickers of longing, an endless delight.

We sip on the stories, sip on the past,
Each frosty flicker a treasure so vast.
Through seasons of sorrow, and moments of grace,
Nostalgia's light flickers, a constant embrace.

Enchanted Lightfall

When shadows beckon, and daylight fades,
The world grows still, in twilight's raids.
Enchanted whispers float on the breeze,
Carrying dreams through the rustling trees.

Golden hues spill, like liquid gold,
Painting the sky, soft stories told.
Lightfall dances, in a gentle grace,
A symphony woven, time can't erase.

The stars awake from their slumber deep,
As the land breathes softly, in secrets to keep.
Each shimmer invites us to wander and roam,
Through enchanted paths, we find our home.

With every heartbeat, the night unfolds,
Tales of the ancients, the prayers of the bold.
Here in this moment, the magic ignites,
Enchanted lightfall weaves wondrous nights.

As moonlight embraces, all worries take flight,
In the heart of the night, everything feels right.
In enchanted realms, we are free to explore,
Where lightfall beckons, forevermore.

Aura of the Night Sky

In the canvas above, colors collide,
A shimmering aura, where secrets abide.
Stars paint the darkness with delicate grace,
A tapestry woven, in cosmic embrace.

Nebulas flicker, like whispers in time,
The heartbeat of worlds, in rhythm and rhyme.
An aura of wonder, twinkling so bright,
Guides dreamers' hearts through the velvety night.

The moon, a lantern, casting soft beams,
Illuminating paths where the dreamer gleams.
In silence we wander, through vast open space,
Captured by beauty in each star's embrace.

Galaxies swirl, in a cosmic ballet,
Cradling the wishes we dare not betray.
Caught in the aura, we dance with delight,
Under the blanket of the mystical night.

In this celestial realm, our spirits take flight,
With an aura of stars, everything feels right.
Let us cherish the beauty that skies can bestow,
An infinite journey, where dreams gently flow.

Chasing the Northern Lights

In the stillness of night, they dance,
Colors swirling, a fleeting chance.
Green and violet brush the sky,
A cosmic ballet, soaring high.

Footsteps crunch on frosty ground,
A silent thrill, magic found.
Eyes lifted, hearts ignite,
In awe beneath the celestial light.

Whispers weave among the trees,
Nature's breath carried by the breeze.
Each shimmer tells a timeless tale,
In this wonder, we prevail.

The darkness cradles our dreams,
As the starlit canvas beams.
Chasing thoughts on frigid air,
We find ourselves, a bond so rare.

With every flash, we feel alive,
In this moment, we truly thrive.
Northern lights guide our way,
A journey etched in night and day.

Illuminated Silence

In the hush where shadows blend,
Light breaks softly, a gentle friend.
Whispers linger in the glow,
Secrets of the night bestow.

Stars hang like dreams on velvet skies,
Illuminated truth, where silence lies.
Each flicker, a heart's desire,
In calm embrace, we rise higher.

Moonlit paths beckon us near,
Shimmering hopes, we hold dear.
Time stands still in this embrace,
Each moment cherished, a sacred space.

The world outside drifts far away,
In illuminated silence, we stay.
Life's chaos fades to a gentle hum,
In the peaceful glow, we become.

Underneath this radiant dome,
We find solace, we feel at home.
With hearts aglow, we intertwine,
In this silence, love's design.

Glacial Dreams

Frozen whispers in the air,
Crystal visions, wonders rare.
Mountains rise, a silent call,
In icy realms, we feel so small.

Glacial dreams shimmer bright,
A world awash in purest light.
Each flake dances, a fleeting sight,
A tapestry woven in the night.

Footprints trail in snowy white,
Guiding us toward the light.
Every breath, a frosty sigh,
As we reach for the endless sky.

Amidst this realm of solitude,
We find warmth in gratitude.
A moment suspended, we hold dear,
In glacial dreams, we conquer fear.

The beauty of stillness, pure and grand,
In this frigid world, hand in hand.
Embracing time, a perfect gleam,
In our hearts, those glacial dreams.

Soft Beams in the Dark

In the shadows where dreams awake,
Soft beams flicker, hopes quake.
They weave through night with gentle grace,
Illuminating every space.

A lantern hue, a guiding star,
Whispers echo from afar.
In every beam, a story told,
Of love and warmth, a heart of gold.

Moonlight pours through branches bare,
Casting spells upon the air.
In twilight's arms, the world transforms,
A dance of light as night conforms.

These soft beams cradle our fear,
Chasing away the darkness near.
With every glow, we rise anew,
In their comfort, dreams break through.

As night unfolds, we learn to see,
The beauty in simplicity.
Soft beams in the dark impart,
A gentle light within the heart.

Glistening Whispers

In the quiet of the night,
Stars gleam with a soft delight.
Whispers float on the breeze,
Carried through the swaying trees.

Moonlight dances on the ground,
Echoes of magic all around.
Each glimmer holds a tale,
Of secret wonders beyond the pale.

Silver shadows fall and rise,
Underneath the jeweled skies.
Nature sings a gentle tune,
As dreams are woven by the moon.

Time slows to a gentle pause,
Life wraps in its quiet laws.
In glistening moments we find,
Beauty for the heart and mind.

Every flicker tells a thought,
In the stillness, wisdom's sought.
In whispers soft, we awaken,
To the magic long unshaken.

Frost-Misted Dreams

In the dawn's tender embrace,
Frost paints the world, a shimmering lace.
Each blade of grass, a glistening pearl,
Reflecting whispers of winter's swirl.

Dreams drift softly on the air,
With every breath, a frosty prayer.
Nature's breath upon the glass,
Moments pause as seasons pass.

Icicles hang like crystal chandeliers,
Marking time with thawing tears.
In the chill, stories unfold,
Of warmth and wonders to behold.

As the sun begins to rise,
Colors dance in morning skies.
Frost-misted dreams will fade away,
But memories linger, here to stay.

Hope shines bright in icy frames,
As life awakens, calling names.
Each heartbeat sings a new refrain,
In the dance of frost and gain.

A Tapestry of Light

Threads of gold and hues so bright,
Weave together in the night.
Patterns glow with soft allure,
A tapestry that feels so pure.

Each stitch binds a story told,
Of lovers, tales both young and old.
Across the fabric, shadows play,
Illuminating the hidden way.

Glimmers twine in gentle grace,
Every hue finds its place.
In this world where colors blend,
A symphony that has no end.

Stars join in the woven dance,
Within their glow, we find a chance.
To see the beauty all around,
In the vibrant threads of sound.

Life's a canvas, vast and wide,
With every heartbeat, we decide.
To craft our own unique design,
In a tapestry that feels divine.

Charms Beneath the Ice

Beneath the frozen, wintry veil,
Lies a magic in every trail.
Charms awaken with the thaw,
Nature's secrets fill with awe.

Crystals form in pure delight,
Glistening softly in the light.
Each flake whispers, tells a tale,
Of journeys past on a silver sail.

As the world begins to melt,
Every charm and dream is felt.
Life stirs deep within the frost,
Finding treasures, never lost.

In the quiet of the thaw,
Beauty thrives without a flaw.
Underneath the ice's grip,
Hope awakens, starts to slip.

With each moment, warmth ignites,
Revealing wonders, hidden sights.
Charms beneath the ice will gleam,
A testament to life's sweet dream.

Glows and Glitches of the Solstice

In the hush of night, shadows play,
Flickering lights chase the gray.
Whispers of warmth in the cold air,
Hints of magic everywhere.

Starry glimmers paint the sky,
As fleeting moments rise and fly.
Caught in the pulse of nature's dance,
We find our hearts lost in the trance.

Echoes of dreams drift near and far,
Guided by the light of a fragile star.
In this place where time stands still,
We embrace the night, our spirits thrill.

Glitches in light, a fleeting art,
Spark and shimmer, each plays a part.
Resonating deep within the soul,
These moments of magic help us feel whole.

With every glow, stitch time anew,
Solstice magic, fierce and true.
In darkness, we find a spark,
In glows and glitches, we leave our mark.

Winks of Warmth from the Shadows

In the corners where shadows blend,
Soft whispers of warmth do send.
Fleeting smiles in the night,
Elusive, yet, they feel so right.

Moonlight dances on quiet streets,
In the stillness, the heart beats.
Winks of warmth, a gentle tease,
Shadows stir with the evening breeze.

With every step, a story told,
Of secret paths both brave and bold.
Warmth encircles, a soft embrace,
Within the night, we find our place.

Lights flicker like fireflies' wink,
Inviting us to pause and think.
In the shadows, we lose and find,
The layers of the heart and mind.

As the night unfolds its thread,
We gather the warmth, not fear the dread.
For in shadows, love does bloom,
Winks of warmth dispel the gloom.

Light Dances on the Icy Path

Upon the frozen road we tread,
Soft light dances, a gentle spread.
Icy crystals glimmer bright,
As day gives in to the velvet night.

Each step we take leaves a trace,
Glowing patterns, a fleeting grace.
Twinkling stars smile from above,
Illuminating our path with love.

In the silence, laughter rings,
Echoing joy that winter brings.
Light twirls gracefully in the dark,
Awakening dreams with every spark.

Beneath the moon's enchanting gaze,
We wander through this winter maze.
Magic swirls in the frosty chill,
As hearts awaken, the world stands still.

With every shimmer of icy gleam,
We weave together a winter's dream.
On this path where light ignites,
We find our way through coldest nights.

Celestial Glow of Distant Stars

In the canvas of the night sky,
Distant stars wink, oh so high.
Soft whispers from realms afar,
Guiding hearts like a hopeful star.

Dreams take flight on cosmic wings,
In the quiet, the universe sings.
Celestial glow wraps us tight,
A blanket of wonder, pure delight.

Stars shimmer tales of long-lost days,
Reminding us of myriad ways.
Each point of light a story spun,
Of love and loss, of battles won.

As galaxies swirl in a silent dance,
We gaze in wonder, hearts in trance.
The night is alive with a magical spark,
Uniting souls in the celestial dark.

With each heartbeat under the skies,
We feel the whispers, we hear the sighs.
The glow of stars ignites our dreams,
In their embrace, life's mystic seems.

Illuminated Footprints

In twilight's glow, we walk anew,
With dreams like stars in skies so blue.
Tracing paths where shadows play,
Each step a wish that lights the way.

Whispers of time, in silence found,
Marking journeys on sacred ground.
Footprints gleam with tales untold,
Memories warm as the evening unfolds.

Through valleys deep and hills so high,
We chase the echoes, let spirits fly.
Guided by the moon's soft light,
In the heart of darkness, we find our sight.

Every step, a dance we share,
Connected by dreams, a bond so rare.
In the glow of night, we walk with pride,
Illuminated paths, our souls collide.

With each trace of our fleeting years,
We leave behind both hopes and fears.
In every footprint, a story grows,
An endless journey, as the river flows.

The Quiet Radiance

In the hush of dawn, light softly spreads,
Painting the sky where silence treads.
Golden hues seep through the trees,
Unraveling secrets carried by the breeze.

Gentle whispers on the morning air,
Waking moments of tender care.
A tranquil heart finds peace within,
In the quiet glow, new dreams begin.

Glistening dew on blades of grass,
Catching the light, as moments pass.
A canvas brushed with strokes of grace,
Each dawn is a gift we embrace.

Through the stillness, a call to rise,
Under the vast, expansive skies.
With every heartbeat, a song of hope,
In quiet radiance, we learn to cope.

As shadows fade and day breaks free,
Our hearts ignite with purity.
In the golden glow, we find our way,
The quiet radiance leads the day.

Shimmering Frost

As winter's breath turns night to white,
The world awakens in soft twilight.
Crystals sparkle on branches bare,
Whispers of magic linger in the air.

Footsteps crunch on the frosty ground,
Each sound a melody, a soothing sound.
Nature's blanket, pure and bright,
A canvas of dreams in the soft moonlight.

The trees wear coats of glimmering ice,
Each branch adorned like nature's spice.
A hush falls deep, serene and clear,
In shimmering frost, the world draws near.

Under the stars, cold kisses land,
Silent wonders, nature's hand.
In winter's glow, we find delight,
Shimmering frost, a heartwarming sight.

In each frosty breath, a story thrives,
Of seasons changing, of vibrant lives.
With every glimmer, we dream and dare,
In shimmering frost, our hope laid bare.

Heartbeats Beneath the Snow

Under layers of soft, white snow,
Life pulses gently, a quiet flow.
Hidden dreams in slumber's embrace,
Awaiting the sun and spring's warm face.

Roots entwined in the frozen earth,
Whispers of life, a silent birth.
Through the cold, the heart beats strong,
In the depths of winter, where we belong.

Each flake that falls, a note so pure,
Composing songs of love, secure.
In the stillness, we find our way,
Heartbeats beneath the snowy sway.

As seasons shift and shadows fade,
Time will unveil the dreams we've made.
With every thaw, a heartbeat sings,
Of life reborn in the warmth of springs.

So let the snow cover all we know,
For beneath it stirs a tale of growth.
In nature's hush, we feel the glow,
Of heartbeats beneath the snow.

Glow in the Hallowed Night

Beneath the stars, a whisper sings,
The moon's soft light, a veil that clings.
Shadows dance with gentle grace,
In hallowed night, time finds its place.

A lantern's glow, a lover's sigh,
Chasing dreams as they drift by.
Each flicker holds a tale untold,
In this realm, our hearts unfold.

Echoes of laughter in the dark,
Fleeting moments, a silent spark.
Wrapped in night's tender embrace,
We find solace, a sacred space.

Stars may fade, but love remains,
Through velvet skies, it gently reigns.
Together we weave through shadows' flight,
As we glow in the hallowed night.

So let us cherish this twilight hour,
A sanctuary, a rare flower.
In every heartbeat, the world is bright,
Together, we glow in the hallowed night.

Twilight's Clarity

When day gives way to evening's sway,
A canvas painted in shades of gray.
Soft whispers float on the cooling breeze,
As nature's voice begins to tease.

The horizon blushes, a gentle hue,
Promising secrets, ancient and new.
In twilight's glow, all things align,
Moments captured, perfectly divine.

A call of the night, a bird in flight,
Chasing shadows in fading light.
With every heartbeat, clarity blooms,
In serene spaces, the spirit resumes.

The stars awaken, one by one,
Bathing the world in silver sun.
As darkness lingers and dreams take flight,
We find our peace in twilight's light.

So here we stand, together still,
Embracing the magic, the quiet thrill.
In twilight's arms, our hearts ignite,
Finding hope in the softest light.

Crystal Illumination

Glistening shards of purest night,
Reflecting dreams, drawing in light.
Through forest paths, where fairies tread,
Crystal shadows dance overhead.

In the stillness, a whisper gleams,
Illuminating all our dreams.
With every step on this sacred ground,
Mysteries of the heart are found.

Sparkling dew on the grass does lie,
A thousand stars in the canvas sky.
Each drop a promise, each gleam a sign,
In crystal illumination, so divine.

Let the moon be our guiding star,
Leading us softly, no matter how far.
In the quiet, our spirits play,
Illuminated by night's ballet.

So take my hand, as we float and sway,
In this world of wonder where we shall stay.
With hearts aglow, destined to shine,
In crystal illumination, you are mine.

Signs of the Night Sky

Beneath the vast expanse, we gaze,
Tracing constellations, lost in a maze.
Each star a marker of dreams once spun,
In the quiet, we become one.

The night sky whispers of ages past,
Tales of love and woe that last.
Guided by starlight, we seek our way,
Finding solace as shadows play.

Planets dance in a rhythmic waltz,
Each twinkle a promise, no faults.
With every breath, the universe flows,
In signs of the night sky, our spirit grows.

So lift your eyes, let the magic stir,
Feel the heartbeat of night as it purrs.
Together we'll wander, hand in hand,
Reading the signs that the heavens have planned.

For life's a journey, mysterious and bright,
In the tapestry woven with stars of the night.
In their glow, we find our truth,
Under the signs of the night sky, eternal youth.

Silent Glow of Solstice

In the hush where shadows sway,
Whispers of the night hold sway,
Stars emerge with subtle grace,
Casting dreams in quiet space.

Moonbeams dance on silver streams,
Glimmers caught in soft night dreams,
Silent wishes carried far,
Beneath the gentle guiding star.

Nature breathes a breath so still,
Echoing the night's heart's thrill,
Time slows down, a tender flow,
In the silent glow of solstice glow.

Memory calls like an old friend,
In this stillness, troubles mend,
Time drifts softly as hearts know,
Peace resides in silent glow.

Softer skies, the world retreats,
In the night, the spirit meets,
Every sigh, a tender vow,
In the silence of the now.

Carried by the Night Air

Underneath a sky so wide,
Silent wishes often hide,
Stars like lanterns, dimly glow,
Carried forth by night's soft flow.

Breeze that whispers through the trees,
Brings the past upon the breeze,
Secrets float like dreams unsure,
Echoes linger, soft and pure.

So the night air hums its song,
Melodies that linger long,
Thoughts that drift like clouds in flight,
Carried softly on the night.

Traces of a day now ceased,
In this calm, the heart finds peace,
Soft caress of evening's breath,
Carried whispers hint at death.

Every moment gently sways,
In the night where silence plays,
Hopes take wing and spirits rise,
Carried by the night's sweet sighs.

Lanterns of Silence

In the stillness, lanterns glow,
Flickering like thoughts that flow,
Guiding shadows, soft and bright,
Through the canvas of the night.

Hushed beneath the starry dome,
Whispers find their way back home,
Lanterns lit with dreams anew,
Casting hope in every hue.

Silent echoes weave their tales,
Memory in every gale,
Fragile lights that gently sway,
Lanterns guide us on our way.

Stillness reigns as time unfolds,
Every secret softly told,
The heart listens, calm, devout,
Lanterns show what life's about.

In the quiet moments spread,
Hope ignites where fears have fled,
Love ignites the darkest night,
Lanterns shine with purest light.

Illuminated Tranquility

In twilight's grasp, the world decays,
Wrapped in calm of gentle ways,
Softly gleaming, peace takes flight,
Illuminated by the night.

Stars emerge with soft delight,
Guiding hearts through cool twilight,
Every breath a silent plea,
In this space, the soul feels free.

Shadows dance with fleeting grace,
In the still, they find their place,
Underneath this vast expanse,
Illuminated, dreams shall prance.

Whispers of the dusk arise,
Cradling thoughts beneath the skies,
In their hold, the world shall see,
Tranquility sets spirits free.

Surrendering to twilight's glow,
Hearts unite, and love will show,
In the silence, beauty reigns,
Illuminated, life remains.

Frigid Embrace

In the stillness of the night,
Whispers dance on icy air,
Wrapped in winter's curfew tight,
Hearts find warmth in silent prayer.

Snowflakes swirl like dreams unfurled,
Casting shadows on the ground,
In this cold and haunting world,
Love's soft touch can still be found.

Branches clothed in crystal sheen,
Echoes of a distant song,
Nature's beauty, pure and keen,
In the frost, we feel we belong.

Beneath the moon's ethereal gaze,
Every breath a clouded mist,
In the stillness, we are swayed,
Holding onto moments kissed.

Through the chill, our spirits rise,
In the dark, there glimmers hope,
Underneath the starry skies,
Together, we will always cope.

Gleaming in the Gloom

In shadows deep, the light will play,
Glistening dreams allure the night,
Flickers of hope in disarray,
Guide us through this fading sight.

Within the depths of silent fears,
Stars become our guiding flames,
Shattering the weight of years,
Whispers echo, calling names.

A shimmer breaks the darkened veil,
Casting sparks on weary souls,
Every heartbeat tells a tale,
Of love and loss and distant goals.

With every pulse, we resurrect,
Glimmers thriving in the void,
Binding us as we connect,
In the night, we find our joy.

So face the gloom with open mind,
For in the dark, the light will bloom,
Through tangled paths, our hearts aligned,
We'll shine like stars, dispelling doom.

Frostbite's Embrace

Chilled by whispers of the night,
Fingers numb, yet spirits soar,
In the frost, we search for light,
Breath suspended, hearts explore.

Each step crunches through the snow,
Echoes of the past reside,
Memories in crystals glow,
Guiding paths we love to stride.

A silver blanket drapes the land,
Frozen dreams in slumber lie,
Nature's palette, vast and grand,
Calling us to dare and fly.

With every gust, the chill invites,
Whispers of the winter's tale,
In the dark, our hope ignites,
Together, we shall brave the gale.

So let the frostbite steal our breath,
Revealing treasures spirits chase,
In the dance of life and death,
We find our warmth in frosty grace.

Sparkling Serenity

Amidst the calm of twilight's glow,
Laughter lingers on the breeze,
Nature's peace, a gentle flow,
Whispers carried through the trees.

Stars alight in gentle grace,
Painting skies with silver dreams,
In this still and sacred space,
Life emerges in radiant streams.

Each moment shines, a fleeting gift,
Like dew upon the morning grass,
In this serene and tender rift,
Time slows down, and sorrows pass.

With every breath, we find our place,
In harmony with earth and sky,
Embracing all that we embrace,
In the stillness, spirits fly.

Through shadows deep, our hearts will sail,
Guided by the moon's sweet light,
In sparkling peace, we'll never fail,
Finding joy in silent night.

Stardust in the Snow

Whispers of winter fall softly low,
A blanket of beauty, where memories flow.
Crystals that twinkle, so pure and bright,
Dancing like dreams in the soft moonlight.

Footsteps of silence, secrets they keep,
Footprints entwined in the hush of sleep.
Sparkling wonders, each flake unique,
A quiet enchantment, a world mystique.

Stars overhead, a celestial show,
Painting the heavens, a stunning glow.
Winds weave a tale of frost and delight,
In this frozen canvas, pure and white.

Voices of nature, a soft, gentle hum,
Echoing softly, where winter winds drum.
Under the starlight, a moment we share,
Stardust in snowflakes, a beauty rare.

Cherish the magic, embrace the glow,
In the heart of winter, love does grow.
Where stardust lingers, memories sew,
In the arms of the night, life's sweet tableau.

Glow of the Evergreens

Beneath the canopy, shadows play,
Evergreens whisper, guiding the way.
A tapestry woven with branches so wide,
Nature's embrace, where dreams can abide.

Soft golden beams through needles will glide,
Casting long shadows where fairies confide.
A trail of fresh pine, a scent in the breeze,
Bringing sweet solace, a heart's gentle ease.

Under the boughs, solace we find,
A moment to breathe, leaving worries behind.
With each rustling leaf, tales come alive,
In the stillness of nature, our spirits revive.

The glow of the evergreens sparkles anew,
Baskets of memories, both old and true.
Together we wander, together we roam,
In the heart of the woods, we find our home.

Dancing in sunlight, shadows entwined,
In the glow of the evergreens, peace is aligned.
Nature's lullaby, forever it sings,
In the whispers of green, life's promise springs.

Solstice Reflections

Amidst the twilight, day stretches long,
The turning of seasons, where we belong.
Candles are lit, a warm, tender glow,
As we gather 'round in the soft sunset's flow.

Memories flourish like leaves in the breeze,
Moments reflected, we savor with ease.
Laughter and stories, echoes of past,
Binding us closer, this joy will last.

The solstice beckons, nature's embrace,
With each gentle whisper, a warm trace.
Turning of worlds, the cycle goes round,
In the hearth of our hearts, true warmth can be found.

Marking the moments, a dance in the light,
Celebrating shadows that blend into night.
A tapestry woven with threads of our lives,
In the laughter of loved ones, our spirit thrives.

As stars awaken, we carry the glow,
In the silence of night, our spirits can grow.
Solstice reflections, a gift we embrace,
With hope in our hearts, we celebrate grace.

Silent Glow of the Night

In the hush of the evening, a whisper is born,
Wrapped in a velvet, where dreams are worn.
The stars oversee, a celestial light,
Guiding lost hearts through the silent night.

Moonlight cascades on the fields of gold,
Stories of magic in shadows retold.
Each glance at the sky, a moment divine,
In the stillness of night, our spirits align.

Dreams dance like fireflies, soft in their flight,
Painting the canvas of the endless night.
In the quiet glow, peace finds its way,
Guide us through dark, till the break of day.

Wrapped in the stillness, we pause and reflect,
In the silent glow, our hearts reconnect.
Every heartbeat echoes, a soft serenade,
In the shadows of night, true magic is made.

Beneath the vast heavens, we find our place,
In the silent glow, we embrace the grace.
Together we wander, beneath stars that gleam,
In the silence of night, we cradle our dreams.

Nightfall's Glow

The sun slips low, a tender sigh,
Across the sky, the colors fly.
Whispers of night begin to weave,
In darkness deep, our dreams believe.

Stars awaken with twinkling light,
Guiding the way through the velvet night.
Moonlight dances on silver streams,
Igniting hearts with whispered dreams.

Trees stand tall in shadows cast,
Embracing secrets of the past.
Crickets play their soft serenade,
In the stillness, memories fade.

Each breeze carries a gentle tune,
Rustling leaves beneath the moon.
Nightfall's glow, a calming balm,
Wrapping the world in soothing calm.

As darkness deepens, hope ignites,
In the embrace of starry nights.
We close our eyes, the journey starts,
With nightfall's glow, we mend our hearts.

Whispering Flakes

Caught in a dance, they twirl and sway,
Whispering flake, the gentle ballet.
Falling softly from skies above,
A silent song of winter's love.

Each flake tells tales of frosty seas,
Drifting lightly with wintry breeze.
Together they blanket the earth in white,
Transforming the world, a wondrous sight.

Children laugh, as snowballs fly,
Underneath the vast, dark sky.
With every flake, a story spins,
In this realm where magic begins.

Crisp air carries the scent of pine,
While stars peek through, their lights align.
As night descends, the flakes aglow,
In a hush, they fall, a whispered flow.

Dancing dreams on winter's breath,
Gentle reminders of life and death.
Whispering flakes, with love and grace,
Nestle the world in a soft embrace.

Candlelight in the Snow

A flicker warms the chill outside,
As snowflakes gather, soft and wide.
Candlelight glows with amber hues,
Casting shadows as it snoozes.

Homes wrapped tight with gentle light,
Embrace the night, a tranquil sight.
Each flame whispers of hope and cheer,
While winter's breath draws close and near.

Outside, the world is crisp and white,
Inside, we gather, hearts alight.
Stories shared by candle's glow,
Binding us close as cold winds blow.

Through frosted panes, we watch the fall,
A shimmering quilt, embracing all.
In the warmth, we find our peace,
With candlelight, the worries cease.

The night drapes soft, in beauty's glow,
While candles flicker, secrets flow.
In snowy realms, love shall stay,
Candlelight guides the night away.

Shimmering Shadows

Beneath the moon, the shadows play,
In shimmering hues, they glide away.
Elusive forms that twist and turn,
In every flicker, passions burn.

Trees stretch tall against the night,
Casting whispers in silver light.
With every step, a dance unfolds,
A mystery made of stories told.

Crickets sing a lullaby sweet,
While shadows gather, dark and fleet.
In the quiet, secrets blend,
Where twilight whispers, hearts will mend.

Stars above join in the waltz,
Their shimmer bright, with none to fault.
Shadows shimmer, a wraith-like song,
Leading us where we feel we belong.

As night deepens, we find our way,
In shimmering shadows, love will stay.
Bound by dreams and soft lament,
In shadows' arms, our nights are spent.

Luminous Frost

In the hush of the night, whispers gleam,
Frosted branches in a silvery dream.
Stars twinkle softly in a velvet sky,
While the cold winds softly sigh.

Footprints crunch on a path of white,
Moonlight dances, a shimmering light.
Each breath a cloud in the frigid air,
Nature sleeps in enchanted despair.

Crystals form where the shadows play,
Painting the world in icy ballet.
A cloak of silence wraps the land,
As winter's touch, gentle and grand.

Tree limbs adorned with their frozen lace,
Time seems to pause in this tranquil space.
The stillness a balm for the weary soul,
In the magic of frost, we feel whole.

Morning breaks with a golden hue,
Sparkling frost that glitters anew.
With each ray of light, the world awakes,
As the beauty of winter quietly breaks.

Enchanted Chill

In twilight's embrace, shadows grow long,
A melody whispers, a cold, haunting song.
The autumn leaves dance in the brisk air,
Nature's breath mingles with magic's rare.

Frost paints the windows with intricate art,
Silent wonders ignite in the heart.
Each moment a treasure, unwrapped with care,
As the chill of the season winds through our hair.

Icicles hanging, a crystalline gleam,
Reflections of whispers caught in a dream.
Under the moonlight, the world holds its breath,
In the stillness of night, we beckon sweet death.

A fire's warm glow in the hearth draws us near,
While the winds carry secrets we long to hear.
Stories of ages, of frost and of flame,
In the heart of the chill, we find life's true name.

The scent of pine fills the frosty air,
As an enchanted chill wraps us with care.
Nature's song echoes, a soft lullaby,
In the tender embrace of the winter sky.

Ember-Draped Nights

Embers glow softly, a warm, gentle light,
Casting shadows that dance in the night.
The crackle of wood, a familiar sound,
As warmth wraps around, comfort is found.

Stars peek through clouds, a twinkling choir,
Filling the heavens with ancient fire.
Each wish we whisper, carried away,
On the breath of the night, where dreams gently sway.

Beneath the vast sky, our spirits take flight,
In the still of the moment, everything feels right.
Memories linger like smoke in the air,
Filling our hearts with a tender care.

The chill of the evening melts with a sigh,
As laughter and stories beneath starlit sky.
Wrapped in cocoon of friendship and love,
We find our warmth in the stars up above.

Through ember-draped nights, we lovingly roam,
With hearts intertwined, we discover our home.
In the glow of the fire, our souls ignite bright,
Each moment a spark, in the silence of night.

The Magic of the Solstice

In the season's turn, the longest night,
Stars gather 'round in a dazzling sight.
A hush falls softly, time seems to freeze,
In the heart of the dark, we find our peace.

Whispers of legends dance on the breeze,
Carried on wings of ancient trees.
As the world holds its breath, anticipation grows,
For the magic of solstice, the light it bestows.

Candles flicker, casting shadows long,
With each flame ignited, we share a song.
Celebrating light as it slowly returns,
In the warmth of the fire, our spirit yearns.

The earth cradles secrets, both old and wise,
In the darkness, we find the brightest skies.
With hearts wide open, we dance with the night,
As the magic of solstice ignites our delight.

Gathered together, our laughter rings clear,
Bound by the warmth, the joy we hold dear.
In the cycle of life, as shadows expand,
We celebrate light, hand in hand, we stand.